# CHICKEN HATCHING LOG BOOK

*Hatching baby chicks is so exciting! It's an awesome experience to watch this miracle for everyone involved. I have hatched eggs several times, and decided to create a log book to better track day 1-21.... Hatch day!*

*This log includes room for the start date (this is always important to keep track of!), reminders to keep track of the temperature and humidity, and a space to write in the time you turn the eggs, if you don't have an automatic egg turner on your incubator.*

*This is just a simple log book to aid you in chick hatching. There are LOTS of books and YouTube video's to assist you on your incubation adventures and raising chicks. I highly recommend doing lots of research before you begin.*

*Happy Hatching!*

*Amy C.*
*(aka: The Crazy Chicken Lady)*

## DON'T COUNT YOUR CHICKENS BEFORE THEY HATCH!

# CHICKEN EGG INCUBATION TIPS

* Choose clean, fertilized eggs that are less than 10 days old to incubate.

* Place your incubator in a draft free room out of direct sunlight.

* Turn your incubator on the day before you plan on putting in the eggs. Check the temperature several times to make sure it stays a consistent 99.5 degrees for forced air and 101-102 for a still air incubator.

* Keep the humidity in the incubator between 40-50% for the first 18 days. If your incubator doesn't have an egg turner, you will have to manually turn eggs 3-5 times a day.

* Candle eggs after 8 days of incubation. I use a flashlight in a dark room. You should see a darkened blob with what looks like veins, or a red spider web at this time.

* Dispose of any eggs that are not developing and mark eggs with a pencil if unsure

* Candle eggs again around day 15, and dispose bad eggs.

* On day 18, stop turning the eggs. Remove the automatic turner if you have one. Raise the humidity in the incubator by adding water to the reservoir or by adding a wet sponge. You will want the humidity at 65-70% during this time.

* Days 18-24 the incubator is on "lock down". Opening the incubator during this time can let out too much humidity and will dry out the membrane of the hatching chicks and can cause them to get stuck (shrink wrapped) in their shells. Resist the urge to open the incubator if you can help it.

* Around day 21, the chicks will start pipping. Pipping is when they peck a hole in their egg shell with their little egg tooth on their beak. You might hear them cheeping even before they pip. They will slowly peck their way around the shell in a circle all the way around. This is called zipping. After they are unzipped, they will push off the top of the egg and pop out.

* Hatches can be different. Sometimes they hatch quickly and other times it can take up to 24 hours.

* Leave chicks in the incubator until they are dry and fluffy, and all hatched out.

* Move chicks to the brooder, and clean your incubator well to remove all debris and bacteria.

# CHICKEN HATCHING LOG

**START DATE:** _____  **EXPECTED HATCH DATE:** _____  **NUMBER OF EGGS:** _____

TEMPERATURE: 99.5° FOR CIRCULATED AIR INCUBATORS (101° FOR STILL AIR INCUBATORS) HUMIDITY: 45-50%

HUMIDITY: 65-70%

| DAY # | TURN EGGS | CHECK HUMIDITY & TEMPERATURE | TURN EGGS | TURN EGGS |
|---|---|---|---|---|
| DAY BEFORE | Clean and plug in incubator, add water and adjust temperature until it is a steady 99.5°, and humidity is 45-50%. Leave on. | | | |
| DAY 1 | ADD EGGS! Do not start turning until day 2 (If using an automatic egg turner, do not turn eggs) | | | |
| DAY 2 | | | | |
| DAY 3 | | | | |
| DAY 4 | | | | |
| DAY 5 | | | | |
| DAY 6 | | | | |
| DAY 7 | | | | |
| DAY 8 | CANDLE THE EGGS (Remove any that aren't growing) | | | |
| | | | | |
| DAY 9 | | | | |
| DAY 10 | | | | |
| DAY 11 | | | | |
| DAY 12 | | | | |
| DAY 13 | | | | |
| DAY 14 | | | | |
| DAY 15 | CANDLE THE EGGS (Remove any that aren't growing) | | | |
| | | | | |
| DAY 16 | | | | |
| DAY 17 | | | | |
| DAY 18 | ADD WATER FOR 65-70% HUMIDITY. STOP TURNING EGGS. If using an automatic turner, remove it from incubator at this time. | | | |
| DAY 19 | You may start to hear chicks peep! Listen closely! | | | |
| DAY 20 | Watch eggs for movement and pipping! | | | |
| HATCH DAY | Enjoy watching chicks hatch! Happy Birthday chicks! | | | |

**NUMBER OF CHICKS HATCHED:** _____  **HATCH RATE % :** _____

# CHICKEN SCRATCHES
## (SKETCHES AND NOTES)

# 🐣 CHICKEN HATCHING LOG 🐣

**START DATE:** _____  **EXPECTED HATCH DATE:** _____  **NUMBER OF EGGS:** _____

*TEMPERATURE: 99.5° FOR CIRCULATED AIR INCUBATORS (101° FOR STILL AIR INCUBATORS) HUMIDITY: 45-50%*

*HUMIDITY: 65-70%*

| DAY # | TURN EGGS | CHECK HUMIDITY & TEMPERATURE | TURN EGGS | TURN EGGS |
|---|---|---|---|---|
| DAY BEFORE | Clean and plug in incubator, add water and adjust temperature until it is a steady 99.5°, and humidity is 45-50%. Leave on. | | | |
| DAY 1 | ADD EGGS! Do not start turning until day 2 (If using an automatic egg turner, do not turn eggs) | | | |
| DAY 2 | | | | |
| DAY 3 | | | | |
| DAY 4 | | | | |
| DAY 5 | | | | |
| DAY 6 | | | | |
| DAY 7 | | | | |
| DAY 8 | CANDLE THE EGGS (Remove any that aren't growing) | | | |
| | | | | |
| DAY 9 | | | | |
| DAY 10 | | | | |
| DAY 11 | | | | |
| DAY 12 | | | | |
| DAY 13 | | | | |
| DAY 14 | | | | |
| DAY 15 | CANDLE THE EGGS (Remove any that aren't growing) | | | |
| | | | | |
| DAY 16 | | | | |
| DAY 17 | | | | |
| DAY 18 | ADD WATER FOR 65-70% HUMIDITY. STOP TURNING EGGS. If using an automatic turner, remove it from incubator at this time. | | | |
| DAY 19 | You may start to hear chicks peep! Listen closely! | | | |
| DAY 20 | Watch eggs for movement and pipping! | | | |
| HATCH DAY | Enjoy watching chicks hatch! Happy Birthday chicks! | | | |

**NUMBER OF CHICKS HATCHED:** _____  **HATCH RATE % :** _____

# CHICKEN SCRATCHES

## (SKETCHES AND NOTES)

# CHICKEN HATCHING LOG

**START DATE:** _____ **EXPECTED HATCH DATE:** _____ **NUMBER OF EGGS:** _____

| DAY # | TURN EGGS | CHECK HUMIDITY & TEMPERATURE | TURN EGGS | TURN EGGS |
|---|---|---|---|---|
| DAY BEFORE | Clean and plug in incubator, add water and adjust temperature until it is a steady 99.5°, and humidity is 45-50%. Leave on. | | | |
| DAY 1 | ADD EGGS! Do not start turning until day 2 (If using an automatic egg turner, do not turn eggs) | | | |
| DAY 2 | | | | |
| DAY 3 | | | | |
| DAY 4 | | | | |
| DAY 5 | | | | |
| DAY 6 | | | | |
| DAY 7 | | | | |
| DAY 8 | CANDLE THE EGGS (Remove any that aren't growing) | | | |
| | | | | |
| DAY 9 | | | | |
| DAY 10 | | | | |
| DAY 11 | | | | |
| DAY 12 | | | | |
| DAY 13 | | | | |
| DAY 14 | | | | |
| DAY 15 | CANDLE THE EGGS (Remove any that aren't growing) | | | |
| | | | | |
| DAY 16 | | | | |
| DAY 17 | | | | |
| DAY 18 | ADD WATER FOR 65-70% HUMIDITY. STOP TURNING EGGS. If using an automatic turner, remove it from incubator at this time. | | | |
| DAY 19 | You may start to hear chicks peep! Listen closely! | | | |
| DAY 20 | Watch eggs for movement and pipping! | | | |
| HATCH DAY | Enjoy watching chicks hatch! Happy Birthday chicks! | | | |

*(Left margin)* TEMPERATURE: 99.5° FOR CIRCULATED AIR INCUBATORS (101° FOR STILL AIR INCUBATORS) HUMIDITY: 45-50%

*(Left margin)* HUMIDITY: 65-70%

**NUMBER OF CHICKS HATCHED:** _____ **HATCH RATE % :** _____

# CHICKEN SCRATCHES
## (SKETCHES AND NOTES)

# CHICKEN HATCHING LOG

**START DATE:** _____  **EXPECTED HATCH DATE:** _____  **NUMBER OF EGGS:** _____

| DAY # | TURN EGGS | CHECK HUMIDITY & TEMPERATURE | TURN EGGS | TURN EGGS |
|---|---|---|---|---|
| DAY BEFORE | Clean and plug in incubator, add water and adjust temperature until it is a steady 99.5°, and humidity is 45-50%. Leave on. | | | |
| DAY 1 | ADD EGGS! Do not start turning until day 2 (If using an automatic egg turner, do not turn eggs) | | | |
| DAY 2 | | | | |
| DAY 3 | | | | |
| DAY 4 | | | | |
| DAY 5 | | | | |
| DAY 6 | | | | |
| DAY 7 | | | | |
| DAY 8 | CANDLE THE EGGS (Remove any that aren't growing) | | | |
| | | | | |
| DAY 9 | | | | |
| DAY 10 | | | | |
| DAY 11 | | | | |
| DAY 12 | | | | |
| DAY 13 | | | | |
| DAY 14 | | | | |
| DAY 15 | CANDLE THE EGGS (Remove any that aren't growing) | | | |
| | | | | |
| DAY 16 | | | | |
| DAY 17 | | | | |
| DAY 18 | ADD WATER FOR 65-70% HUMIDITY. STOP TURNING EGGS. If using an automatic turner, remove it from incubator at this time. | | | |
| DAY 19 | You may start to hear chicks peep! Listen closely! | | | |
| DAY 20 | Watch eggs for movement and pipping! | | | |
| HATCH DAY | Enjoy watching chicks hatch! Happy Birthday chicks! | | | |

*TEMPERATURE: 99.5° FOR CIRCULATED AIR INCUBATORS (101° FOR STILL AIR INCUBATORS) HUMIDITY: 45-50%*

*HUMIDITY: 65-70%*

**NUMBER OF CHICKS HATCHED:** _____  **HATCH RATE % :** _____

# CHICKEN SCRATCHES

## (SKETCHES AND NOTES)

# ☙ CHICKEN HATCHING LOG ☙

**START DATE:** _____  **EXPECTED HATCH DATE:** _____  **NUMBER OF EGGS:** _____

| DAY # | TURN EGGS | CHECK HUMIDITY & TEMPERATURE | TURN EGGS | TURN EGGS |
|---|---|---|---|---|
| DAY BEFORE | Clean and plug in incubator, add water and adjust temperature until it is a steady 99.5°, and humidity is 45-50%. Leave on. | | | |
| DAY 1 | ADD EGGS! Do not start turning until day 2 (If using an automatic egg turner, do not turn eggs) | | | |
| DAY 2 | | | | |
| DAY 3 | | | | |
| DAY 4 | | | | |
| DAY 5 | | | | |
| DAY 6 | | | | |
| DAY 7 | | | | |
| DAY 8 | CANDLE THE EGGS (Remove any that aren't growing) | | | |
| | | | | |
| DAY 9 | | | | |
| DAY 10 | | | | |
| DAY 11 | | | | |
| DAY 12 | | | | |
| DAY 13 | | | | |
| DAY 14 | | | | |
| DAY 15 | CANDLE THE EGGS (Remove any that aren't growing) | | | |
| | | | | |
| DAY 16 | | | | |
| DAY 17 | | | | |
| DAY 18 | ADD WATER FOR 65-70% HUMIDITY. STOP TURNING EGGS. If using an automatic turner, remove it from incubator at this time. | | | |
| DAY 19 | You may start to hear chicks peep! Listen closely! | | | |
| DAY 20 | Watch eggs for movement and pipping! | | | |
| HATCH DAY | **Enjoy watching chicks hatch! Happy Birthday chicks!** | | | |

TEMPERATURE: 99.5° FOR CIRCULATED AIR INCUBATORS (101° FOR STILL AIR INCUBATORS) HUMIDITY: 45-50%

HUMIDITY: 65-70%

**NUMBER OF CHICKS HATCHED:** _____  **HATCH RATE % :** _____

# CHICKEN SCRATCHES
## (SKETCHES AND NOTES)

# CHICKEN HATCHING LOG

**START DATE:** _____  **EXPECTED HATCH DATE:** _____  **NUMBER OF EGGS:** _____

| DAY # | TURN EGGS | CHECK HUMIDITY & TEMPERATURE | TURN EGGS | TURN EGGS |
|---|---|---|---|---|
| DAY BEFORE | Clean and plug in incubator, add water and adjust temperature until it is a steady 99.5°, and humidity is 45-50%. Leave on. | | | |
| DAY 1 | ADD EGGS! Do not start turning until day 2 (If using an automatic egg turner, do not turn eggs) | | | |
| DAY 2 | | | | |
| DAY 3 | | | | |
| DAY 4 | | | | |
| DAY 5 | | | | |
| DAY 6 | | | | |
| DAY 7 | | | | |
| DAY 8 | CANDLE THE EGGS (Remove any that aren't growing) | | | |
| | | | | |
| DAY 9 | | | | |
| DAY 10 | | | | |
| DAY 11 | | | | |
| DAY 12 | | | | |
| DAY 13 | | | | |
| DAY 14 | | | | |
| DAY 15 | CANDLE THE EGGS (Remove any that aren't growing) | | | |
| | | | | |
| DAY 16 | | | | |
| DAY 17 | | | | |
| DAY 18 | ADD WATER FOR 65-70% HUMIDITY. STOP TURNING EGGS. If using an automatic turner, remove it from incubator at this time. | | | |
| DAY 19 | You may start to hear chicks peep! Listen closely! | | | |
| DAY 20 | Watch eggs for movement and pipping! | | | |
| HATCH DAY | Enjoy watching chicks hatch! Happy Birthday chicks! | | | |

TEMPERATURE: 99.5° FOR CIRCULATED AIR INCUBATORS (101° FOR STILL AIR INCUBATORS) HUMIDITY: 45-50%

HUMIDITY: 65-70%

**NUMBER OF CHICKS HATCHED:** _____  **HATCH RATE % :** _____

# CHICKEN SCRATCHES
## (SKETCHES AND NOTES)

# CHICKEN HATCHING LOG

**START DATE:** _____ **EXPECTED HATCH DATE:** _____ **NUMBER OF EGGS:** _____

| DAY # | TURN EGGS | CHECK HUMIDITY & TEMPERATURE | TURN EGGS | TURN EGGS |
|---|---|---|---|---|
| DAY BEFORE | Clean and plug in incubator, add water and adjust temperature until it is a steady 99.5°, and humidity is 45-50%. Leave on. | | | |
| DAY 1 | ADD EGGS! Do not start turning until day 2 (If using an automatic egg turner, do not turn eggs) | | | |
| DAY 2 | | | | |
| DAY 3 | | | | |
| DAY 4 | | | | |
| DAY 5 | | | | |
| DAY 6 | | | | |
| DAY 7 | | | | |
| DAY 8 | CANDLE THE EGGS (Remove any that aren't growing) | | | |
| | | | | |
| DAY 9 | | | | |
| DAY 10 | | | | |
| DAY 11 | | | | |
| DAY 12 | | | | |
| DAY 13 | | | | |
| DAY 14 | | | | |
| DAY 15 | CANDLE THE EGGS (Remove any that aren't growing) | | | |
| | | | | |
| DAY 16 | | | | |
| DAY 17 | | | | |
| DAY 18 | ADD WATER FOR 65-70% HUMIDITY. STOP TURNING EGGS. If using an automatic turner, remove it from incubator at this time. | | | |
| DAY 19 | You may start to hear chicks peep! Listen closely! | | | |
| DAY 20 | Watch eggs for movement and pipping! | | | |
| HATCH DAY | Enjoy watching chicks hatch! Happy Birthday chicks! | | | |

**TEMPERATURE: 99.5° FOR CIRCULATED AIR INCUBATORS (101° FOR STILL AIR INCUBATORS) HUMIDITY: 45-50%**

**HUMIDITY: 65-70%**

**NUMBER OF CHICKS HATCHED:** _____ **HATCH RATE % :** _____

# CHICKEN SCRATCHES
## (SKETCHES AND NOTES)

# CHICKEN HATCHING LOG

**START DATE:** _____ **EXPECTED HATCH DATE:** _____ **NUMBER OF EGGS:** _____

| DAY # | TURN EGGS | CHECK HUMIDITY & TEMPERATURE | TURN EGGS | TURN EGGS |
|---|---|---|---|---|
| DAY BEFORE | Clean and plug in incubator, add water and adjust temperature until it is a steady 99.5°, and humidity is 45-50%. Leave on. | | | |
| DAY 1 | ADD EGGS! Do not start turning until day 2 (If using an automatic egg turner, do not turn eggs) | | | |
| DAY 2 | | | | |
| DAY 3 | | | | |
| DAY 4 | | | | |
| DAY 5 | | | | |
| DAY 6 | | | | |
| DAY 7 | | | | |
| DAY 8 | CANDLE THE EGGS (Remove any that aren't growing) | | | |
| | | | | |
| DAY 9 | | | | |
| DAY 10 | | | | |
| DAY 11 | | | | |
| DAY 12 | | | | |
| DAY 13 | | | | |
| DAY 14 | | | | |
| DAY 15 | CANDLE THE EGGS (Remove any that aren't growing) | | | |
| | | | | |
| DAY 16 | | | | |
| DAY 17 | | | | |
| DAY 18 | ADD WATER FOR 65-70% HUMIDITY. STOP TURNING EGGS. If using an automatic turner, remove it from incubator at this time. | | | |
| DAY 19 | You may start to hear chicks peep! Listen closely! | | | |
| DAY 20 | Watch eggs for movement and pipping! | | | |
| HATCH DAY | Enjoy watching chicks hatch! Happy Birthday chicks! | | | |

**Left margin (top):** TEMPERATURE: 99.5° FOR CIRCULATED AIR INCUBATORS (101° FOR STILL AIR INCUBATORS) HUMIDITY: 45-50%

**Left margin (bottom):** HUMIDITY: 65-70%

**NUMBER OF CHICKS HATCHED:** _____ **HATCH RATE % :** _____

# CHICKEN SCRATCHES

## (SKETCHES AND NOTES)

# 🐣 CHICKEN HATCHING LOG 🐣

**START DATE:** _____  **EXPECTED HATCH DATE:** _____  **NUMBER OF EGGS:** _____

| DAY # | TURN EGGS | CHECK HUMIDITY & TEMPERATURE | TURN EGGS | TURN EGGS |
|---|---|---|---|---|
| DAY BEFORE | Clean and plug in incubator, add water and adjust temperature until it is a steady 99.5°, and humidity is 45-50%. Leave on. | | | |
| DAY 1 | ADD EGGS! Do not start turning until day 2 (If using an automatic egg turner, do not turn eggs) | | | |
| DAY 2 | | | | |
| DAY 3 | | | | |
| DAY 4 | | | | |
| DAY 5 | | | | |
| DAY 6 | | | | |
| DAY 7 | | | | |
| DAY 8 | CANDLE THE EGGS (Remove any that aren't growing) | | | |
| | | | | |
| DAY 9 | | | | |
| DAY 10 | | | | |
| DAY 11 | | | | |
| DAY 12 | | | | |
| DAY 13 | | | | |
| DAY 14 | | | | |
| DAY 15 | CANDLE THE EGGS (Remove any that aren't growing) | | | |
| | | | | |
| DAY 16 | | | | |
| DAY 17 | | | | |
| DAY 18 | ADD WATER FOR 65-70% HUMIDITY. STOP TURNING EGGS. If using an automatic turner, remove it from incubator at this time. | | | |
| DAY 19 | You may start to hear chicks peep! Listen closely! | | | |
| DAY 20 | Watch eggs for movement and pipping! | | | |
| HATCH DAY | Enjoy watching chicks hatch! Happy Birthday chicks! | | | |

*Left margin (top):* TEMPERATURE: 99.5° FOR CIRCULATED AIR INCUBATORS (101° FOR STILL AIR INCUBATORS) HUMIDITY: 45-50%

*Left margin (bottom):* HUMIDITY: 65-70%

**NUMBER OF CHICKS HATCHED:** _____  **HATCH RATE % :** _____

# CHICKEN SCRATCHES

## (SKETCHES AND NOTES)

# CHICKEN HATCHING LOG

START DATE: _____ EXPECTED HATCH DATE: _____ NUMBER OF EGGS: _____

| DAY # | TURN EGGS | CHECK HUMIDITY & TEMPERATURE | TURN EGGS | TURN EGGS |
|---|---|---|---|---|
| DAY BEFORE | Clean and plug in incubator, add water and adjust temperature until it is a steady 99.5°, and humidity is 45-50%. Leave on. | | | |
| DAY 1 | ADD EGGS! Do not start turning until day 2 (If using an automatic egg turner, do not turn eggs) | | | |
| DAY 2 | | | | |
| DAY 3 | | | | |
| DAY 4 | | | | |
| DAY 5 | | | | |
| DAY 6 | | | | |
| DAY 7 | | | | |
| DAY 8 | CANDLE THE EGGS (Remove any that aren't growing) | | | |
| | | | | |
| DAY 9 | | | | |
| DAY 10 | | | | |
| DAY 11 | | | | |
| DAY 12 | | | | |
| DAY 13 | | | | |
| DAY 14 | | | | |
| DAY 15 | CANDLE THE EGGS (Remove any that aren't growing) | | | |
| | | | | |
| DAY 16 | | | | |
| DAY 17 | | | | |
| DAY 18 | ADD WATER FOR 65-70% HUMIDITY. STOP TURNING EGGS. If using an automatic turner, remove it from incubator at this time. | | | |
| DAY 19 | You may start to hear chicks peep! Listen closely! | | | |
| DAY 20 | Watch eggs for movement and pipping! | | | |
| HATCH DAY | Enjoy watching chicks hatch! Happy Birthday chicks! | | | |

TEMPERATURE: 99.5° FOR CIRCULATED AIR INCUBATORS (101° FOR STILL AIR INCUBATORS) HUMIDITY: 45-50%

HUMIDITY: 65-70%

NUMBER OF CHICKS HATCHED: _____ HATCH RATE % : _____

# CHICKEN SCRATCHES

## (SKETCHES AND NOTES)

# CHICKEN HATCHING LOG

START DATE: ____________ EXPECTED HATCH DATE: ____________ NUMBER OF EGGS: __________

TEMPERATURE: 99.5° FOR CIRCULATED AIR INCUBATORS (101° FOR STILL AIR INCUBATORS) HUMIDITY: 45-50%

HUMIDITY: 65-70%

| DAY # | TURN EGGS | CHECK HUMIDITY & TEMPERATURE | TURN EGGS | TURN EGGS |
|---|---|---|---|---|
| DAY BEFORE | Clean and plug in incubator, add water and adjust temperature until it is a steady 99.5°, and humidity is 45-50%. Leave on. | | | |
| DAY 1 | ADD EGGS! Do not start turning until day 2 (If using an automatic egg turner, do not turn eggs) | | | |
| DAY 2 | | | | |
| DAY 3 | | | | |
| DAY 4 | | | | |
| DAY 5 | | | | |
| DAY 6 | | | | |
| DAY 7 | | | | |
| DAY 8 | CANDLE THE EGGS (Remove any that aren't growing) | | | |
| | | | | |
| DAY 9 | | | | |
| DAY 10 | | | | |
| DAY 11 | | | | |
| DAY 12 | | | | |
| DAY 13 | | | | |
| DAY 14 | | | | |
| DAY 15 | CANDLE THE EGGS (Remove any that aren't growing) | | | |
| | | | | |
| DAY 16 | | | | |
| DAY 17 | | | | |
| DAY 18 | ADD WATER FOR 65-70% HUMIDITY. STOP TURNING EGGS. If using an automatic turner, remove it from incubator at this time. | | | |
| DAY 19 | You may start to hear chicks peep! Listen closely! | | | |
| DAY 20 | Watch eggs for movement and pipping! | | | |
| HATCH DAY | **Enjoy watching chicks hatch! Happy Birthday chicks!** | | | |

NUMBER OF CHICKS HATCHED: __________ HATCH RATE % : ____________

# CHICKEN SCRATCHES

## (SKETCHES AND NOTES)

# CHICKEN HATCHING LOG

**START DATE:** _____ **EXPECTED HATCH DATE:** _____ **NUMBER OF EGGS:** _____

| DAY # | TURN EGGS | CHECK HUMIDITY & TEMPERATURE | TURN EGGS | TURN EGGS |
|---|---|---|---|---|
| DAY BEFORE | Clean and plug in incubator, add water and adjust temperature until it is a steady 99.5°, and humidity is 45-50%. Leave on. | | | |
| DAY 1 | ADD EGGS! Do not start turning until day 2 (If using an automatic egg turner, do not turn eggs) | | | |
| DAY 2 | | | | |
| DAY 3 | | | | |
| DAY 4 | | | | |
| DAY 5 | | | | |
| DAY 6 | | | | |
| DAY 7 | | | | |
| DAY 8 | CANDLE THE EGGS (Remove any that aren't growing) | | | |
| | | | | |
| DAY 9 | | | | |
| DAY 10 | | | | |
| DAY 11 | | | | |
| DAY 12 | | | | |
| DAY 13 | | | | |
| DAY 14 | | | | |
| DAY 15 | CANDLE THE EGGS (Remove any that aren't growing) | | | |
| | | | | |
| DAY 16 | | | | |
| DAY 17 | | | | |
| DAY 18 | ADD WATER FOR 65-70% HUMIDITY. STOP TURNING EGGS. If using an automatic turner, remove it from incubator at this time. | | | |
| DAY 19 | You may start to hear chicks peep! Listen closely! | | | |
| DAY 20 | Watch eggs for movement and pipping! | | | |
| HATCH DAY | Enjoy watching chicks hatch! Happy Birthday chicks! | | | |

**TEMPERATURE: 99.5° FOR CIRCULATED AIR INCUBATORS (101° FOR STILL AIR INCUBATORS) HUMIDITY: 45-50%**

**HUMIDITY: 65-70%**

**NUMBER OF CHICKS HATCHED:** _____ **HATCH RATE % :** _____

# CHICKEN SCRATCHES
## (SKETCHES AND NOTES)

# CHICKEN HATCHING LOG

**START DATE:** _____  **EXPECTED HATCH DATE:** _____  **NUMBER OF EGGS:** _____

| DAY # | TURN EGGS | CHECK HUMIDITY & TEMPERATURE | TURN EGGS | TURN EGGS |
|---|---|---|---|---|
| DAY BEFORE | Clean and plug in incubator, add water and adjust temperature until it is a steady 99.5°, and humidity is 45-50%. Leave on. | | | |
| DAY 1 | ADD EGGS! Do not start turning until day 2 (If using an automatic egg turner, do not turn eggs) | | | |
| DAY 2 | | | | |
| DAY 3 | | | | |
| DAY 4 | | | | |
| DAY 5 | | | | |
| DAY 6 | | | | |
| DAY 7 | | | | |
| DAY 8 | CANDLE THE EGGS (Remove any that aren't growing) | | | |
| | | | | |
| DAY 9 | | | | |
| DAY 10 | | | | |
| DAY 11 | | | | |
| DAY 12 | | | | |
| DAY 13 | | | | |
| DAY 14 | | | | |
| DAY 15 | CANDLE THE EGGS (Remove any that aren't growing) | | | |
| | | | | |
| DAY 16 | | | | |
| DAY 17 | | | | |
| DAY 18 | ADD WATER FOR 65-70% HUMIDITY. STOP TURNING EGGS. If using an automatic turner, remove it from incubator at this time. | | | |
| DAY 19 | You may start to hear chicks peep! Listen closely! | | | |
| DAY 20 | Watch eggs for movement and pipping! | | | |
| HATCH DAY | Enjoy watching chicks hatch! Happy Birthday chicks! | | | |

*Left margin:* TEMPERATURE: 99.5° FOR CIRCULATED AIR INCUBATORS (101° FOR STILL AIR INCUBATORS) HUMIDITY: 45-50%

*Left margin:* HUMIDITY: 65-70%

**NUMBER OF CHICKS HATCHED:** _____  **HATCH RATE % :** _____

# CHICKEN SCRATCHES
## (SKETCHES AND NOTES)

# CHICKEN HATCHING LOG

**START DATE:** _____  **EXPECTED HATCH DATE:** _____  **NUMBER OF EGGS:** _____

**TEMPERATURE: 99.5° FOR CIRCULATED AIR INCUBATORS (101° FOR STILL AIR INCUBATORS) HUMIDITY: 45-50%**

**HUMIDITY: 65-70%**

| DAY # | TURN EGGS | CHECK HUMIDITY & TEMPERATURE | TURN EGGS | TURN EGGS |
|---|---|---|---|---|
| DAY BEFORE | Clean and plug in incubator, add water and adjust temperature until it is a steady 99.5°, and humidity is 45-50%. Leave on. | | | |
| DAY 1 | ADD EGGS! Do not start turning until day 2 (If using an automatic egg turner, do not turn eggs) | | | |
| DAY 2 | | | | |
| DAY 3 | | | | |
| DAY 4 | | | | |
| DAY 5 | | | | |
| DAY 6 | | | | |
| DAY 7 | | | | |
| DAY 8 | CANDLE THE EGGS (Remove any that aren't growing) | | | |
| | | | | |
| DAY 9 | | | | |
| DAY 10 | | | | |
| DAY 11 | | | | |
| DAY 12 | | | | |
| DAY 13 | | | | |
| DAY 14 | | | | |
| DAY 15 | CANDLE THE EGGS (Remove any that aren't growing) | | | |
| | | | | |
| DAY 16 | | | | |
| DAY 17 | | | | |
| DAY 18 | ADD WATER FOR 65-70% HUMIDITY. STOP TURNING EGGS. If using an automatic turner, remove it from incubator at this time. | | | |
| DAY 19 | You may start to hear chicks peep! Listen closely! | | | |
| DAY 20 | Watch eggs for movement and pipping! | | | |
| HATCH DAY | Enjoy watching chicks hatch! Happy Birthday chicks! | | | |

**NUMBER OF CHICKS HATCHED:** _____  **HATCH RATE % :** _____

# CHICKEN SCRATCHES

## (SKETCHES AND NOTES)

# CHICKEN HATCHING LOG

**START DATE:** _____ **EXPECTED HATCH DATE:** _____ **NUMBER OF EGGS:** _____

**TEMPERATURE: 99.5° FOR CIRCULATED AIR INCUBATORS (101° FOR STILL AIR INCUBATORS) HUMIDITY: 45-50%**

**HUMIDITY: 65-70%**

| DAY # | TURN EGGS | CHECK HUMIDITY & TEMPERATURE | TURN EGGS | TURN EGGS |
|---|---|---|---|---|
| DAY BEFORE | Clean and plug in incubator, add water and adjust temperature until it is a steady 99.5°, and humidity is 45-50%. Leave on. | | | |
| DAY 1 | ADD EGGS! Do not start turning until day 2 (If using an automatic egg turner, do not turn eggs) | | | |
| DAY 2 | | | | |
| DAY 3 | | | | |
| DAY 4 | | | | |
| DAY 5 | | | | |
| DAY 6 | | | | |
| DAY 7 | | | | |
| DAY 8 | CANDLE THE EGGS (Remove any that aren't growing) | | | |
| | | | | |
| DAY 9 | | | | |
| DAY 10 | | | | |
| DAY 11 | | | | |
| DAY 12 | | | | |
| DAY 13 | | | | |
| DAY 14 | | | | |
| DAY 15 | CANDLE THE EGGS (Remove any that aren't growing) | | | |
| | | | | |
| DAY 16 | | | | |
| DAY 17 | | | | |
| DAY 18 | ADD WATER FOR 65-70% HUMIDITY. STOP TURNING EGGS. If using an automatic turner, remove it from incubator at this time. | | | |
| DAY 19 | You may start to hear chicks peep! Listen closely! | | | |
| DAY 20 | Watch eggs for movement and pipping! | | | |
| HATCH DAY | Enjoy watching chicks hatch! Happy Birthday chicks! | | | |

**NUMBER OF CHICKS HATCHED:** _____ **HATCH RATE % :** _____

# CHICKEN SCRATCHES

## (SKETCHES AND NOTES)

#  CHICKEN HATCHING LOG

**START DATE:** _____ **EXPECTED HATCH DATE:** _____ **NUMBER OF EGGS:** _____

| DAY # | TURN EGGS | CHECK HUMIDITY & TEMPERATURE | TURN EGGS | TURN EGGS |
|---|---|---|---|---|
| DAY BEFORE | Clean and plug in incubator, add water and adjust temperature until it is a steady 99.5°, and humidity is 45-50%. Leave on. | | | |
| DAY 1 | ADD EGGS! Do not start turning until day 2 (If using an automatic egg turner, do not turn eggs) | | | |
| DAY 2 | | | | |
| DAY 3 | | | | |
| DAY 4 | | | | |
| DAY 5 | | | | |
| DAY 6 | | | | |
| DAY 7 | | | | |
| DAY 8 | CANDLE THE EGGS (Remove any that aren't growing) | | | |
| | | | | |
| DAY 9 | | | | |
| DAY 10 | | | | |
| DAY 11 | | | | |
| DAY 12 | | | | |
| DAY 13 | | | | |
| DAY 14 | | | | |
| DAY 15 | CANDLE THE EGGS (Remove any that aren't growing) | | | |
| | | | | |
| DAY 16 | | | | |
| DAY 17 | | | | |
| DAY 18 | ADD WATER FOR 65-70% HUMIDITY. STOP TURNING EGGS. If using an automatic turner, remove it from incubator at this time. | | | |
| DAY 19 | You may start to hear chicks peep! Listen closely! | | | |
| DAY 20 | Watch eggs for movement and pipping! | | | |
| HATCH DAY | Enjoy watching chicks hatch! Happy Birthday chicks! | | | |

**TEMPERATURE: 99.5° FOR CIRCULATED AIR INCUBATORS (101° FOR STILL AIR INCUBATORS) HUMIDITY: 45-50%**

**HUMIDITY: 65-70%**

**NUMBER OF CHICKS HATCHED:** _____ **HATCH RATE % :** _____

# CHICKEN SCRATCHES

## (SKETCHES AND NOTES)

# 🐣 CHICKEN HATCHING LOG 🐣

**START DATE:** _____ **EXPECTED HATCH DATE:** _____ **NUMBER OF EGGS:** _____

| DAY # | TURN EGGS | CHECK HUMIDITY & TEMPERATURE | TURN EGGS | TURN EGGS |
|---|---|---|---|---|
| DAY BEFORE | Clean and plug in incubator, add water and adjust temperature until it is a steady 99.5°, and humidity is 45-50%. Leave on. | | | |
| DAY 1 | ADD EGGS! Do not start turning until day 2 (If using an automatic egg turner, do not turn eggs) | | | |
| DAY 2 | | | | |
| DAY 3 | | | | |
| DAY 4 | | | | |
| DAY 5 | | | | |
| DAY 6 | | | | |
| DAY 7 | | | | |
| DAY 8 | CANDLE THE EGGS (Remove any that aren't growing) | | | |
| | | | | |
| DAY 9 | | | | |
| DAY 10 | | | | |
| DAY 11 | | | | |
| DAY 12 | | | | |
| DAY 13 | | | | |
| DAY 14 | | | | |
| DAY 15 | CANDLE THE EGGS (Remove any that aren't growing) | | | |
| | | | | |
| DAY 16 | | | | |
| DAY 17 | | | | |
| DAY 18 | ADD WATER FOR 65-70% HUMIDITY. STOP TURNING EGGS. If using an automatic turner, remove it from incubator at this time. | | | |
| DAY 19 | You may start to hear chicks peep! Listen closely! | | | |
| DAY 20 | Watch eggs for movement and pipping! | | | |
| HATCH DAY | Enjoy watching chicks hatch! Happy Birthday chicks! | | | |

*Left margin (top):* TEMPERATURE: 99.5° FOR CIRCULATED AIR INCUBATORS (101° FOR STILL AIR INCUBATORS) HUMIDITY: 45-50%

*Left margin (bottom):* HUMIDITY: 65-70%

**NUMBER OF CHICKS HATCHED:** _____ **HATCH RATE % :** _____

# CHICKEN SCRATCHES
## (SKETCHES AND NOTES)

# CHICKEN HATCHING LOG

**START DATE:** _____  **EXPECTED HATCH DATE:** _____  **NUMBER OF EGGS:** _____

| DAY # | TURN EGGS | CHECK HUMIDITY & TEMPERATURE | TURN EGGS | TURN EGGS |
|---|---|---|---|---|
| DAY BEFORE | Clean and plug in incubator, add water and adjust temperature until it is a steady 99.5°, and humidity is 45-50%. Leave on. | | | |
| DAY 1 | ADD EGGS! Do not start turning until day 2 (If using an automatic egg turner, do not turn eggs) | | | |
| DAY 2 | | | | |
| DAY 3 | | | | |
| DAY 4 | | | | |
| DAY 5 | | | | |
| DAY 6 | | | | |
| DAY 7 | | | | |
| DAY 8 | CANDLE THE EGGS (Remove any that aren't growing) | | | |
| | | | | |
| DAY 9 | | | | |
| DAY 10 | | | | |
| DAY 11 | | | | |
| DAY 12 | | | | |
| DAY 13 | | | | |
| DAY 14 | | | | |
| DAY 15 | CANDLE THE EGGS (Remove any that aren't growing) | | | |
| | | | | |
| DAY 16 | | | | |
| DAY 17 | | | | |
| DAY 18 | ADD WATER FOR 65-70% HUMIDITY. STOP TURNING EGGS. If using an automatic turner, remove it from incubator at this time. | | | |
| DAY 19 | You may start to hear chicks peep! Listen closely! | | | |
| DAY 20 | Watch eggs for movement and pipping! | | | |
| HATCH DAY | Enjoy watching chicks hatch! Happy Birthday chicks! | | | |

TEMPERATURE: 99.5° FOR CIRCULATED AIR INCUBATORS (101° FOR STILL AIR INCUBATORS) HUMIDITY: 45-50%

HUMIDITY: 65-70%

**NUMBER OF CHICKS HATCHED:** _____  **HATCH RATE % :** _____

# CHICKEN SCRATCHES

## (SKETCHES AND NOTES)

# CHICKEN HATCHING LOG

**START DATE:** _____ **EXPECTED HATCH DATE:** _____ **NUMBER OF EGGS:** _____

| DAY # | TURN EGGS | CHECK HUMIDITY & TEMPERATURE | TURN EGGS | TURN EGGS |
|---|---|---|---|---|
| DAY BEFORE | Clean and plug in incubator, add water and adjust temperature until it is a steady 99.5°, and humidity is 45-50%. Leave on. | | | |
| DAY 1 | ADD EGGS! Do not start turning until day 2 (If using an automatic egg turner, do not turn eggs) | | | |
| DAY 2 | | | | |
| DAY 3 | | | | |
| DAY 4 | | | | |
| DAY 5 | | | | |
| DAY 6 | | | | |
| DAY 7 | | | | |
| DAY 8 | CANDLE THE EGGS (Remove any that aren't growing) | | | |
| | | | | |
| DAY 9 | | | | |
| DAY 10 | | | | |
| DAY 11 | | | | |
| DAY 12 | | | | |
| DAY 13 | | | | |
| DAY 14 | | | | |
| DAY 15 | CANDLE THE EGGS (Remove any that aren't growing) | | | |
| | | | | |
| DAY 16 | | | | |
| DAY 17 | | | | |
| DAY 18 | ADD WATER FOR 65-70% HUMIDITY. STOP TURNING EGGS. If using an automatic turner, remove it from incubator at this time. | | | |
| DAY 19 | You may start to hear chicks peep! Listen closely! | | | |
| DAY 20 | Watch eggs for movement and pipping! | | | |
| HATCH DAY | Enjoy watching chicks hatch! Happy Birthday chicks! | | | |

*(Left margin:)* TEMPERATURE: 99.5° FOR CIRCULATED AIR INCUBATORS (101° FOR STILL AIR INCUBATORS) HUMIDITY: 45-50%

*(Left margin lower:)* HUMIDITY: 65-70%

**NUMBER OF CHICKS HATCHED:** _____ **HATCH RATE % :** _____

# CHICKEN SCRATCHES

## (SKETCHES AND NOTES)

# CHICKEN HATCHING LOG

**START DATE:** _____  **EXPECTED HATCH DATE:** _____  **NUMBER OF EGGS:** _____

| DAY # | TURN EGGS | CHECK HUMIDITY & TEMPERATURE | TURN EGGS | TURN EGGS |
|---|---|---|---|---|
| DAY BEFORE | Clean and plug in incubator, add water and adjust temperature until it is a steady 99.5°, and humidity is 45-50%. Leave on. | | | |
| DAY 1 | ADD EGGS! Do not start turning until day 2 (If using an automatic egg turner, do not turn eggs) | | | |
| DAY 2 | | | | |
| DAY 3 | | | | |
| DAY 4 | | | | |
| DAY 5 | | | | |
| DAY 6 | | | | |
| DAY 7 | | | | |
| DAY 8 | CANDLE THE EGGS (Remove any that aren't growing) | | | |
| | | | | |
| DAY 9 | | | | |
| DAY 10 | | | | |
| DAY 11 | | | | |
| DAY 12 | | | | |
| DAY 13 | | | | |
| DAY 14 | | | | |
| DAY 15 | CANDLE THE EGGS (Remove any that aren't growing) | | | |
| | | | | |
| DAY 16 | | | | |
| DAY 17 | | | | |
| DAY 18 | ADD WATER FOR 65-70% HUMIDITY. STOP TURNING EGGS. If using an automatic turner, remove it from incubator at this time. | | | |
| DAY 19 | You may start to hear chicks peep! Listen closely! | | | |
| DAY 20 | Watch eggs for movement and pipping! | | | |
| HATCH DAY | Enjoy watching chicks hatch! Happy Birthday chicks! | | | |

*(Left margin:)* TEMPERATURE: 99.5° FOR CIRCULATED AIR INCUBATORS (101° FOR STILL AIR INCUBATORS) HUMIDITY: 45-50%

*(Left margin lower:)* HUMIDITY: 65-70%

**NUMBER OF CHICKS HATCHED:** _____  **HATCH RATE % :** _____

# CHICKEN SCRATCHES

## (SKETCHES AND NOTES)

# CHICKEN HATCHING LOG

**START DATE:** _____  **EXPECTED HATCH DATE:** _____  **NUMBER OF EGGS:** _____

**TEMPERATURE: 99.5° FOR CIRCULATED AIR INCUBATORS (101° FOR STILL AIR INCUBATORS) HUMIDITY: 45-50%**

**HUMIDITY: 65-70%**

| DAY # | TURN EGGS | CHECK HUMIDITY & TEMPERATURE | TURN EGGS | TURN EGGS |
|---|---|---|---|---|
| DAY BEFORE | Clean and plug in incubator, add water and adjust temperature until it is a steady 99.5°, and humidity is 45-50%. Leave on. | | | |
| DAY 1 | ADD EGGS! Do not start turning until day 2 (If using an automatic egg turner, do not turn eggs) | | | |
| DAY 2 | | | | |
| DAY 3 | | | | |
| DAY 4 | | | | |
| DAY 5 | | | | |
| DAY 6 | | | | |
| DAY 7 | | | | |
| DAY 8 | CANDLE THE EGGS (Remove any that aren't growing) | | | |
| | | | | |
| DAY 9 | | | | |
| DAY 10 | | | | |
| DAY 11 | | | | |
| DAY 12 | | | | |
| DAY 13 | | | | |
| DAY 14 | | | | |
| DAY 15 | CANDLE THE EGGS (Remove any that aren't growing) | | | |
| | | | | |
| DAY 16 | | | | |
| DAY 17 | | | | |
| DAY 18 | ADD WATER FOR 65-70% HUMIDITY. STOP TURNING EGGS. If using an automatic turner, remove it from incubator at this time. | | | |
| DAY 19 | You may start to hear chicks peep! Listen closely! | | | |
| DAY 20 | Watch eggs for movement and pipping! | | | |
| HATCH DAY | Enjoy watching chicks hatch! Happy Birthday chicks! | | | |

**NUMBER OF CHICKS HATCHED:** _____  **HATCH RATE % :** _____

# CHICKEN SCRATCHES

## (SKETCHES AND NOTES)

# ☁ CHICKEN HATCHING LOG ☁

START DATE: _____   EXPECTED HATCH DATE: _____   NUMBER OF EGGS: _____

| DAY # | TURN EGGS | CHECK HUMIDITY & TEMPERATURE | TURN EGGS | TURN EGGS |
|---|---|---|---|---|
| DAY BEFORE | Clean and plug in incubator, add water and adjust temperature until it is a steady 99.5°, and humidity is 45-50%. Leave on. | | | |
| DAY 1 | ADD EGGS! Do not start turning until day 2 (If using an automatic egg turner, do not turn eggs) | | | |
| DAY 2 | | | | |
| DAY 3 | | | | |
| DAY 4 | | | | |
| DAY 5 | | | | |
| DAY 6 | | | | |
| DAY 7 | | | | |
| DAY 8 | CANDLE THE EGGS (Remove any that aren't growing) | | | |
| | | | | |
| DAY 9 | | | | |
| DAY 10 | | | | |
| DAY 11 | | | | |
| DAY 12 | | | | |
| DAY 13 | | | | |
| DAY 14 | | | | |
| DAY 15 | CANDLE THE EGGS (Remove any that aren't growing) | | | |
| | | | | |
| DAY 16 | | | | |
| DAY 17 | | | | |
| DAY 18 | ADD WATER FOR 65-70% HUMIDITY. STOP TURNING EGGS. If using an automatic turner, remove it from incubator at this time. | | | |
| DAY 19 | You may start to hear chicks peep! Listen closely! | | | |
| DAY 20 | Watch eggs for movement and pipping! | | | |
| HATCH DAY | Enjoy watching chicks hatch! Happy Birthday chicks! | | | |

*(Left margin:)* TEMPERATURE: 99.5° FOR CIRCULATED AIR INCUBATORS (101° FOR STILL AIR INCUBATORS) HUMIDITY: 45-50%

*(Left margin:)* HUMIDITY: 65-70%

NUMBER OF CHICKS HATCHED: _____   HATCH RATE % : _____

# CHICKEN SCRATCHES

**(SKETCHES AND NOTES)**

# CHICKEN HATCHING LOG

**START DATE:** _____  **EXPECTED HATCH DATE:** _____  **NUMBER OF EGGS:** _____

| DAY # | TURN EGGS | CHECK HUMIDITY & TEMPERATURE | TURN EGGS | TURN EGGS |
|---|---|---|---|---|
| DAY BEFORE | Clean and plug in incubator, add water and adjust temperature until it is a steady 99.5°, and humidity is 45-50%. Leave on. | | | |
| DAY 1 | ADD EGGS! Do not start turning until day 2 (If using an automatic egg turner, do not turn eggs) | | | |
| DAY 2 | | | | |
| DAY 3 | | | | |
| DAY 4 | | | | |
| DAY 5 | | | | |
| DAY 6 | | | | |
| DAY 7 | | | | |
| DAY 8 | CANDLE THE EGGS (Remove any that aren't growing) | | | |
| | | | | |
| DAY 9 | | | | |
| DAY 10 | | | | |
| DAY 11 | | | | |
| DAY 12 | | | | |
| DAY 13 | | | | |
| DAY 14 | | | | |
| DAY 15 | CANDLE THE EGGS (Remove any that aren't growing) | | | |
| | | | | |
| DAY 16 | | | | |
| DAY 17 | | | | |
| DAY 18 | ADD WATER FOR 65-70% HUMIDITY. STOP TURNING EGGS. If using an automatic turner, remove it from incubator at this time. | | | |
| DAY 19 | You may start to hear chicks peep! Listen closely! | | | |
| DAY 20 | Watch eggs for movement and pipping! | | | |
| HATCH DAY | Enjoy watching chicks hatch! Happy Birthday chicks! | | | |

*TEMPERATURE: 99.5° FOR CIRCULATED AIR INCUBATORS (101° FOR STILL AIR INCUBATORS) HUMIDITY: 45-50%*

*HUMIDITY: 65-70%*

**NUMBER OF CHICKS HATCHED:** _____  **HATCH RATE % :** _____

# CHICKEN SCRATCHES

## (SKETCHES AND NOTES)

# CHICKEN HATCHING LOG

START DATE: _____  EXPECTED HATCH DATE: _____  NUMBER OF EGGS: _____

| DAY # | TURN EGGS | CHECK HUMIDITY & TEMPERATURE | TURN EGGS | TURN EGGS |
|---|---|---|---|---|
| DAY BEFORE | Clean and plug in incubator, add water and adjust temperature until it is a steady 99.5°, and humidity is 45-50%. Leave on. | | | |
| DAY 1 | ADD EGGS! Do not start turning until day 2 (If using an automatic egg turner, do not turn eggs) | | | |
| DAY 2 | | | | |
| DAY 3 | | | | |
| DAY 4 | | | | |
| DAY 5 | | | | |
| DAY 6 | | | | |
| DAY 7 | | | | |
| DAY 8 | CANDLE THE EGGS (Remove any that aren't growing) | | | |
| | | | | |
| DAY 9 | | | | |
| DAY 10 | | | | |
| DAY 11 | | | | |
| DAY 12 | | | | |
| DAY 13 | | | | |
| DAY 14 | | | | |
| DAY 15 | CANDLE THE EGGS (Remove any that aren't growing) | | | |
| | | | | |
| DAY 16 | | | | |
| DAY 17 | | | | |
| DAY 18 | ADD WATER FOR 65-70% HUMIDITY. STOP TURNING EGGS. If using an automatic turner, remove it from incubator at this time. | | | |
| DAY 19 | You may start to hear chicks peep! Listen closely! | | | |
| DAY 20 | Watch eggs for movement and pipping! | | | |
| HATCH DAY | Enjoy watching chicks hatch! Happy Birthday chicks! | | | |

*Left margin: TEMPERATURE: 99.5° FOR CIRCULATED AIR INCUBATORS (101° FOR STILL AIR INCUBATORS) HUMIDITY: 45-50%*

*Left margin lower: HUMIDITY: 65-70%*

NUMBER OF CHICKS HATCHED: _____  HATCH RATE % : _____

# CHICKEN SCRATCHES

## (SKETCHES AND NOTES)

# ☙ CHICKEN HATCHING LOG ☙

**START DATE:** _____ **EXPECTED HATCH DATE:** _____ **NUMBER OF EGGS:** _____

| DAY # | TURN EGGS | CHECK HUMIDITY & TEMPERATURE | TURN EGGS | TURN EGGS |
|-------|-----------|------------------------------|-----------|-----------|
| DAY BEFORE | Clean and plug in incubator, add water and adjust temperature until it is a steady 99.5°, and humidity is 45-50%. Leave on. | | | |
| DAY 1 | ADD EGGS! Do not start turning until day 2 (If using an automatic egg turner, do not turn eggs) | | | |
| DAY 2 | | | | |
| DAY 3 | | | | |
| DAY 4 | | | | |
| DAY 5 | | | | |
| DAY 6 | | | | |
| DAY 7 | | | | |
| DAY 8 | CANDLE THE EGGS (Remove any that aren't growing) | | | |
| | | | | |
| DAY 9 | | | | |
| DAY 10 | | | | |
| DAY 11 | | | | |
| DAY 12 | | | | |
| DAY 13 | | | | |
| DAY 14 | | | | |
| DAY 15 | CANDLE THE EGGS (Remove any that aren't growing) | | | |
| | | | | |
| DAY 16 | | | | |
| DAY 17 | | | | |
| DAY 18 | ADD WATER FOR 65-70% HUMIDITY. STOP TURNING EGGS. If using an automatic turner, remove it from incubator at this time. | | | |
| DAY 19 | You may start to hear chicks peep! Listen closely! | | | |
| DAY 20 | Watch eggs for movement and pipping! | | | |
| HATCH DAY | Enjoy watching chicks hatch! Happy Birthday chicks! | | | |

*Left margin (top):* TEMPERATURE: 99.5° FOR CIRCULATED AIR INCUBATORS (101° FOR STILL AIR INCUBATORS) HUMIDITY: 45-50%

*Left margin (bottom):* HUMIDITY: 65-70%

**NUMBER OF CHICKS HATCHED:** _____ **HATCH RATE % :** _____

# CHICKEN SCRATCHES

(SKETCHES AND NOTES)

# CHICKEN HATCHING LOG

**START DATE:** _____  **EXPECTED HATCH DATE:** _____  **NUMBER OF EGGS:** _____

*(Left margin, top)* TEMPERATURE: 99.5° FOR CIRCULATED AIR INCUBATORS (101° FOR STILL AIR INCUBATORS) HUMIDITY: 45-50%

*(Left margin, bottom)* HUMIDITY: 65-70%

| DAY # | TURN EGGS | CHECK HUMIDITY & TEMPERATURE | TURN EGGS | TURN EGGS |
|---|---|---|---|---|
| DAY BEFORE | Clean and plug in incubator, add water and adjust temperature until it is a steady 99.5°, and humidity is 45-50%. Leave on. | | | |
| DAY 1 | ADD EGGS! Do not start turning until day 2 (If using an automatic egg turner, do not turn eggs) | | | |
| DAY 2 | | | | |
| DAY 3 | | | | |
| DAY 4 | | | | |
| DAY 5 | | | | |
| DAY 6 | | | | |
| DAY 7 | | | | |
| DAY 8 | CANDLE THE EGGS (Remove any that aren't growing) | | | |
| DAY 8 | | | | |
| DAY 9 | | | | |
| DAY 10 | | | | |
| DAY 11 | | | | |
| DAY 12 | | | | |
| DAY 13 | | | | |
| DAY 14 | | | | |
| DAY 15 | CANDLE THE EGGS (Remove any that aren't growing) | | | |
| DAY 15 | | | | |
| DAY 16 | | | | |
| DAY 17 | | | | |
| DAY 18 | ADD WATER FOR 65-70% HUMIDITY. STOP TURNING EGGS. If using an automatic turner, remove it from incubator at this time. | | | |
| DAY 19 | You may start to hear chicks peep! Listen closely! | | | |
| DAY 20 | Watch eggs for movement and pipping! | | | |
| HATCH DAY | Enjoy watching chicks hatch! Happy Birthday chicks! | | | |

**NUMBER OF CHICKS HATCHED:** _____  **HATCH RATE % :** _____

Made in United States
Troutdale, OR
04/06/2025